Womziz

ARCADE GAMER
DOODLE & COLOR BOOK

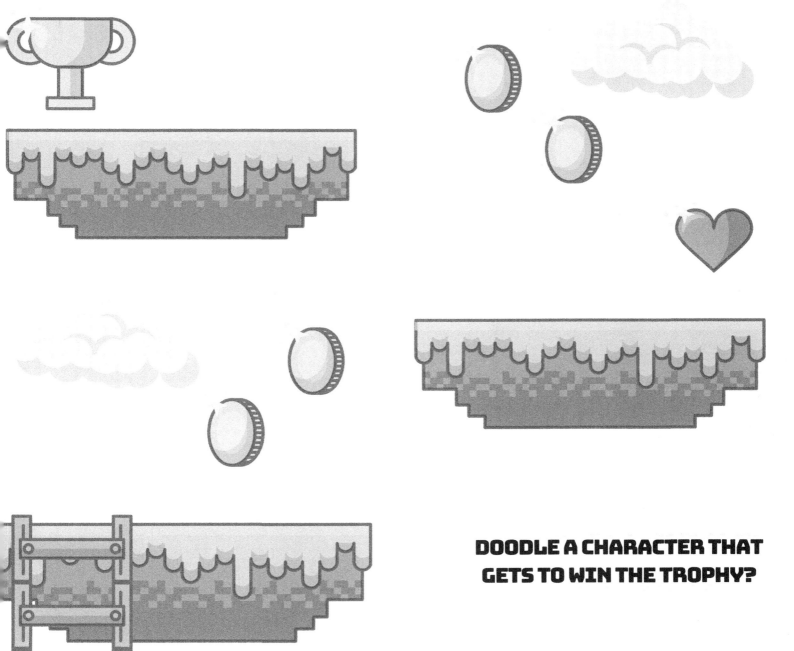

DOODLE A CHARACTER THAT GETS TO WIN THE TROPHY?

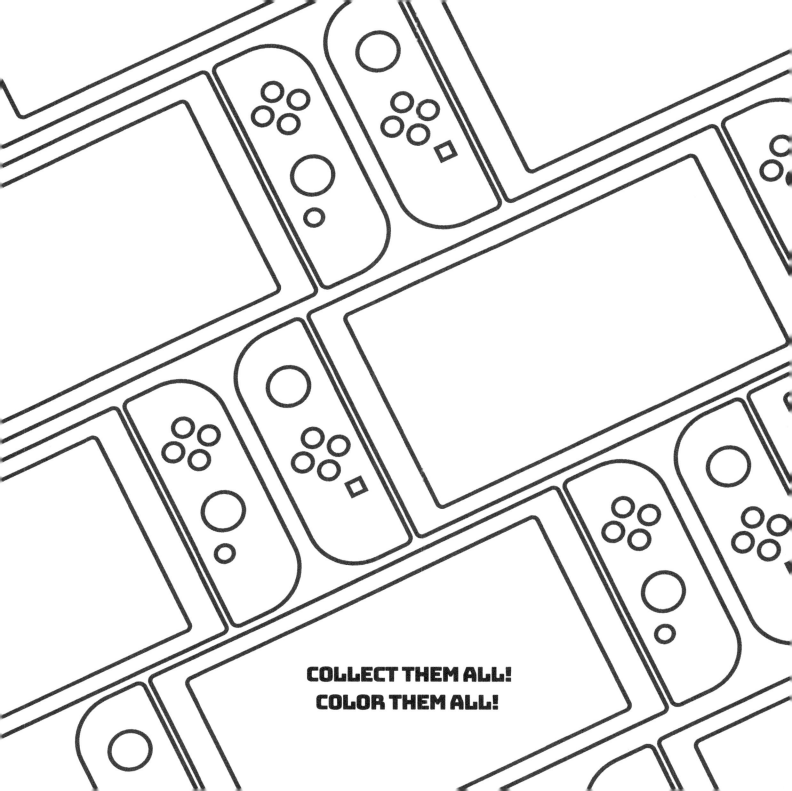

COLLECT THEM ALL!
COLOR THEM ALL!

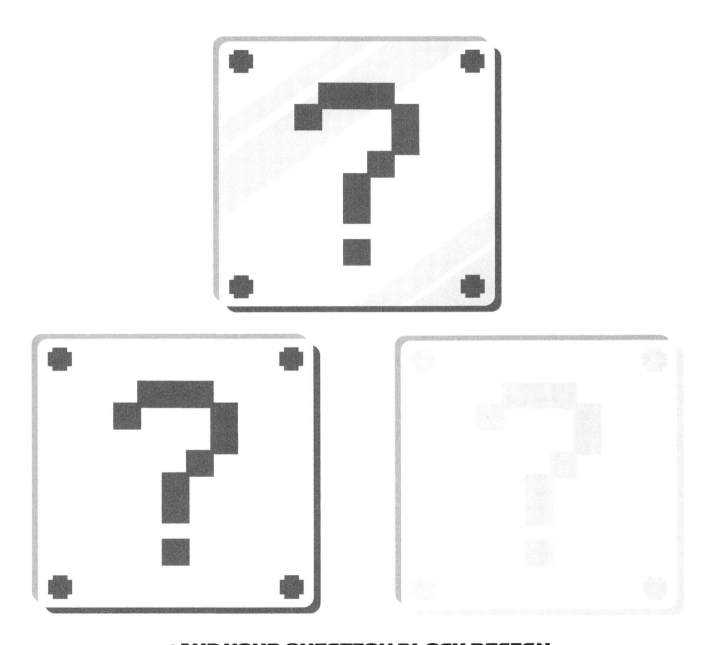

+1UP YOUR QUESTION BLOCK DESIGN

WHAT ARE
YOU PLAYING?

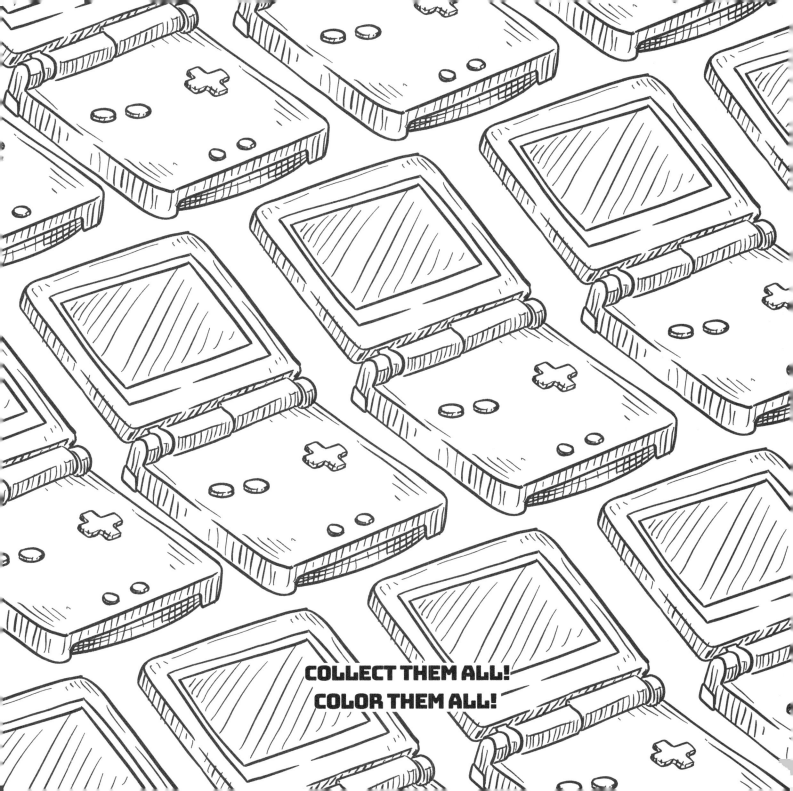

COLLECT THEM ALL!

COLOR THEM ALL!

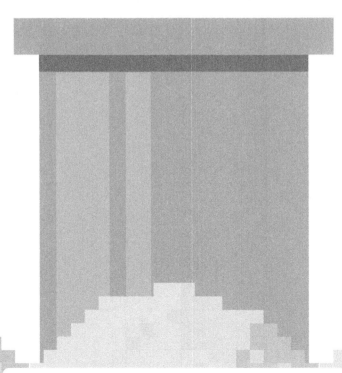

WHAT COMES OUT OF THE PIPE?

CREATE YOUR OWN
2D GAMER LEVEL

LEVEL UP YOUR COLORING!

BEST GAME YOU'VE
EVER PLAYED

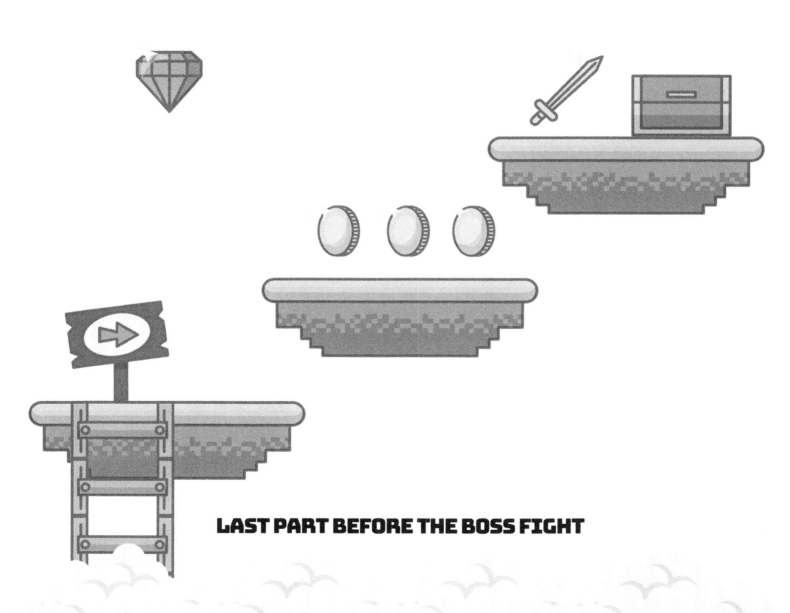

LAST PART BEFORE THE BOSS FIGHT

BOSS FIGHT!!!!!

CONTINUE THE HARDWARE DOODLE

BE A COMPUTER PROGRAMMER AND DOODLE YOUR OWN MINI GAME

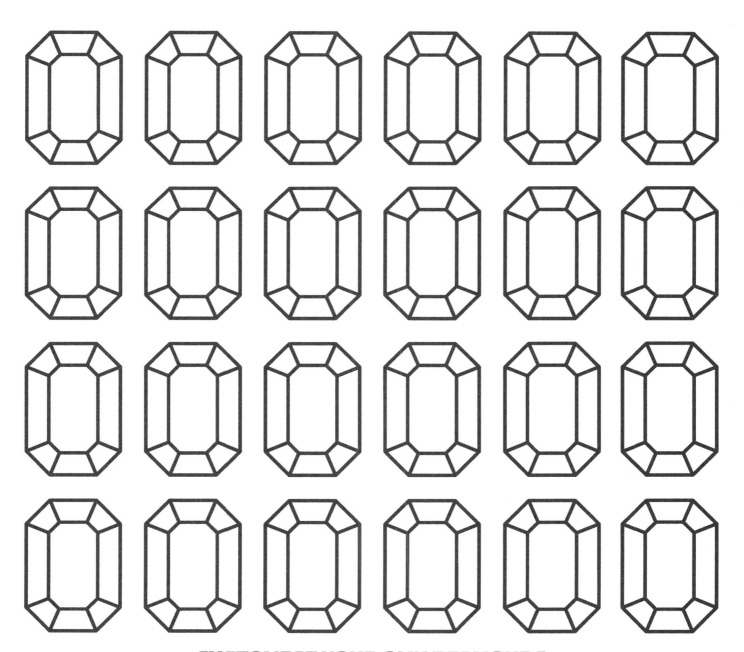

CUSTOMISE YOUR OWN DIAMONDS

+1UP YOUR DOODLES WITH YOUR OWN DESIGN

HIGHLIGHTERS

CONTINUE
THE DOODLE

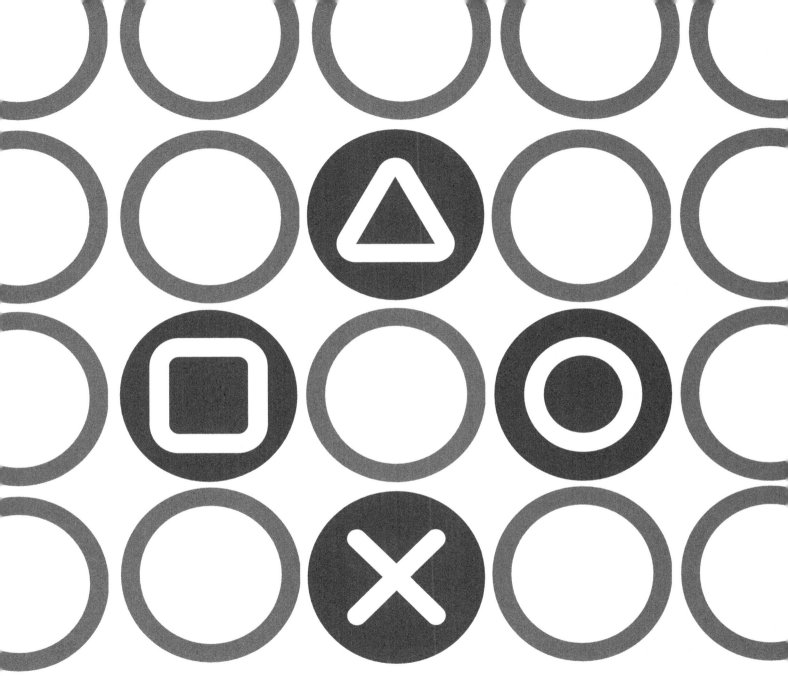

CREATE YOUR OWN BUTTONS

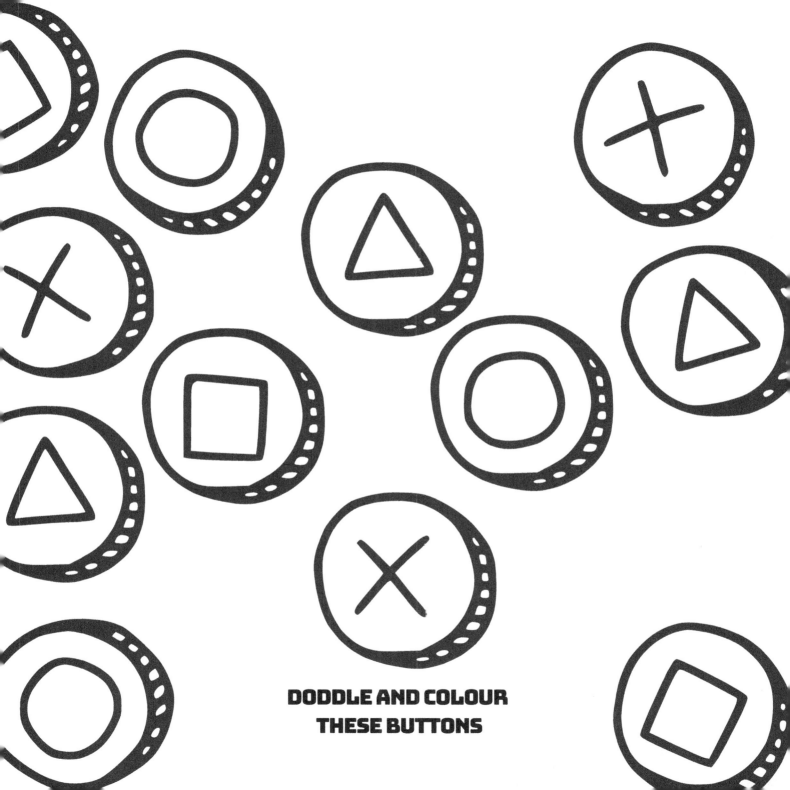

DODDLE AND COLOUR
THESE BUTTONS

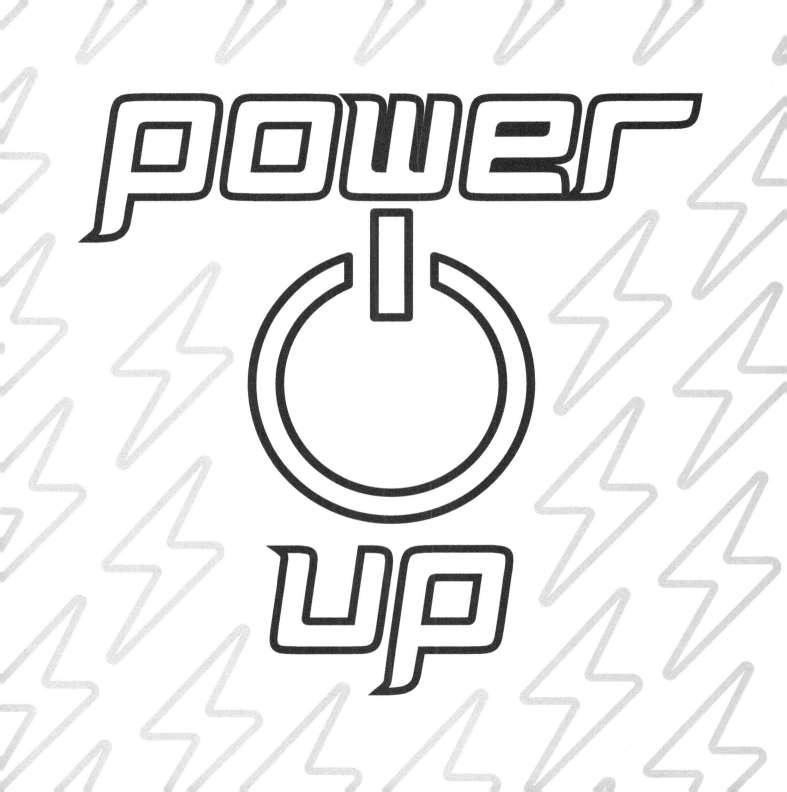

RETRO COLOUR THESE 8-BIT BEAUTIES

COLOUR YOUR OWN TETRIS

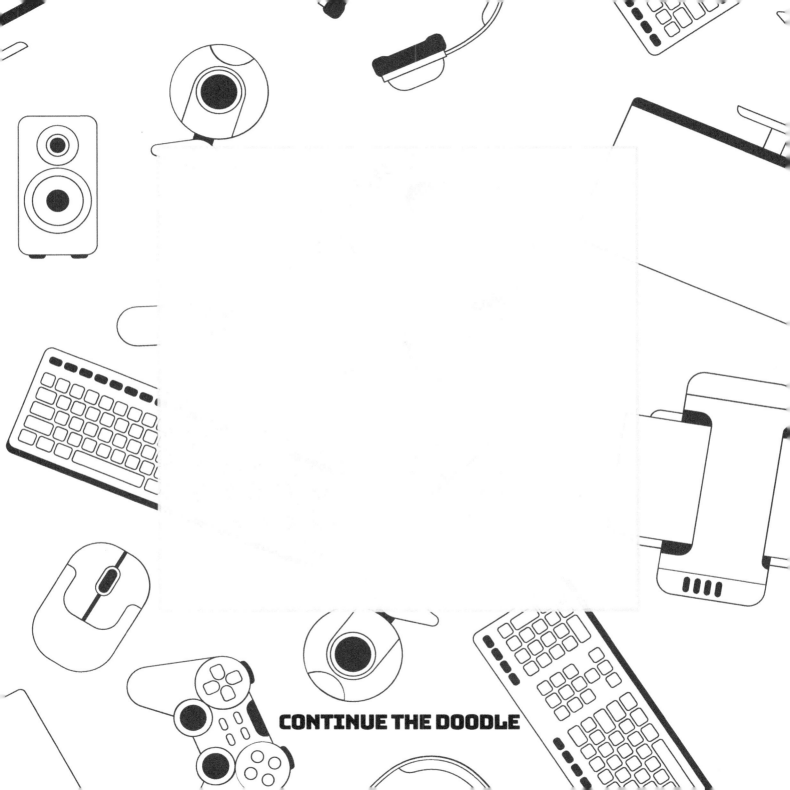

CONTINUE THE DOODLE

DOODLE A WAY TO GET THE HEART

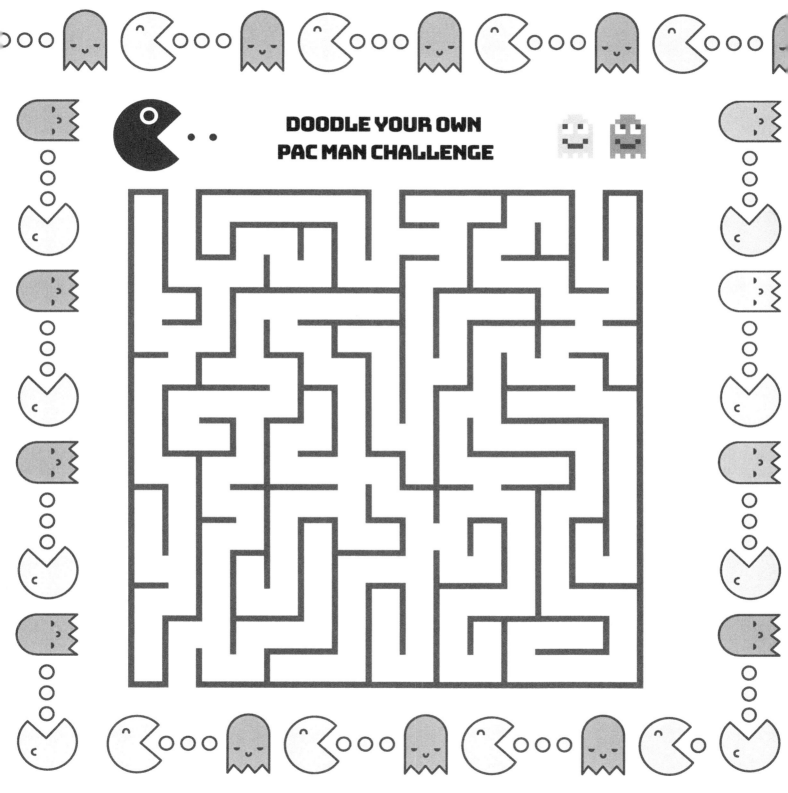

DOODLE YOUR OWN
PAC MAN CHALLENGE

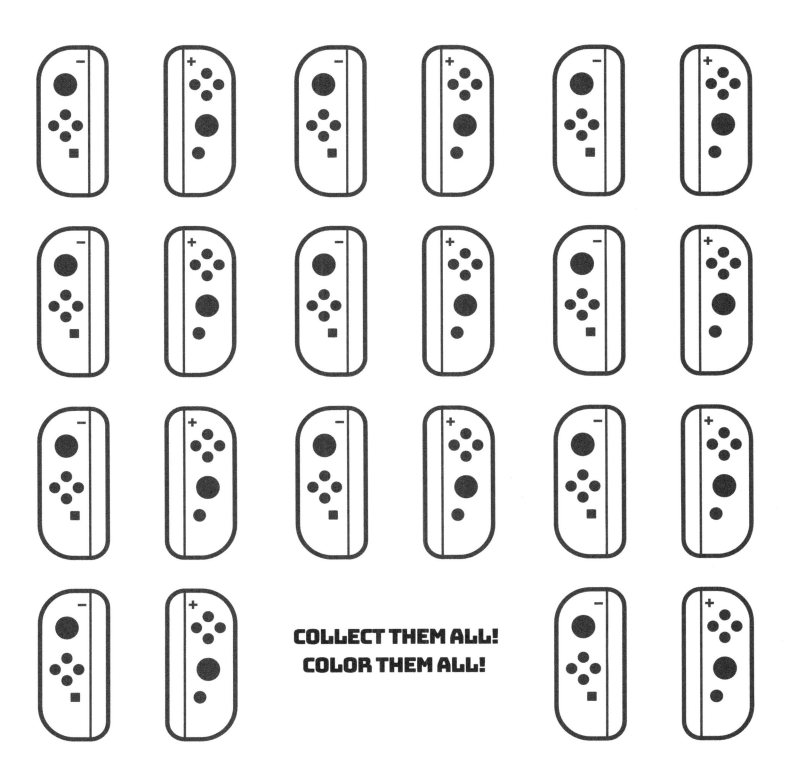

COLLECT THEM ALL!
COLOR THEM ALL!

HIGHLIGHTERS

WHICH CHARACTER GETS A HEALTH BOOST?

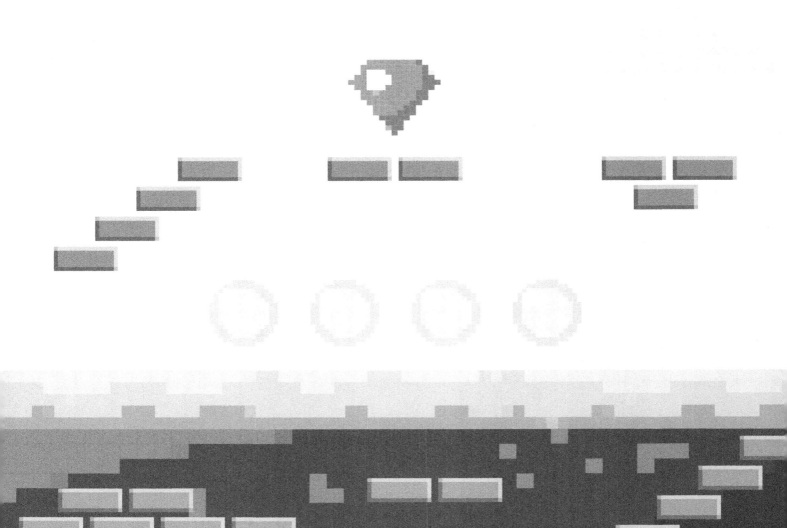

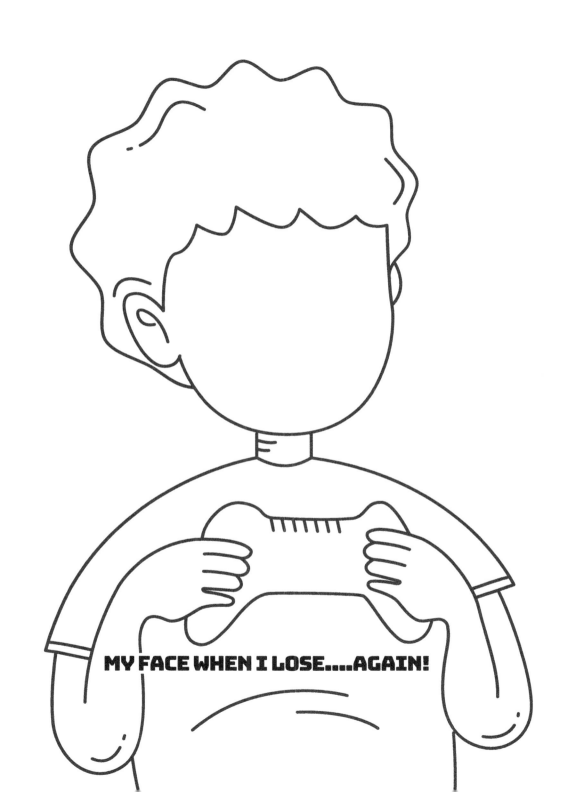

CONTINUE
THE DOODLE

COLLECT THEM ALL!
COLOR THEM ALL!

CREATE YOUR OWN
2D GAMER LEVEL

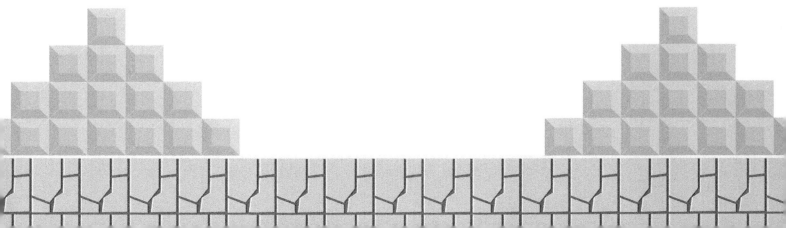

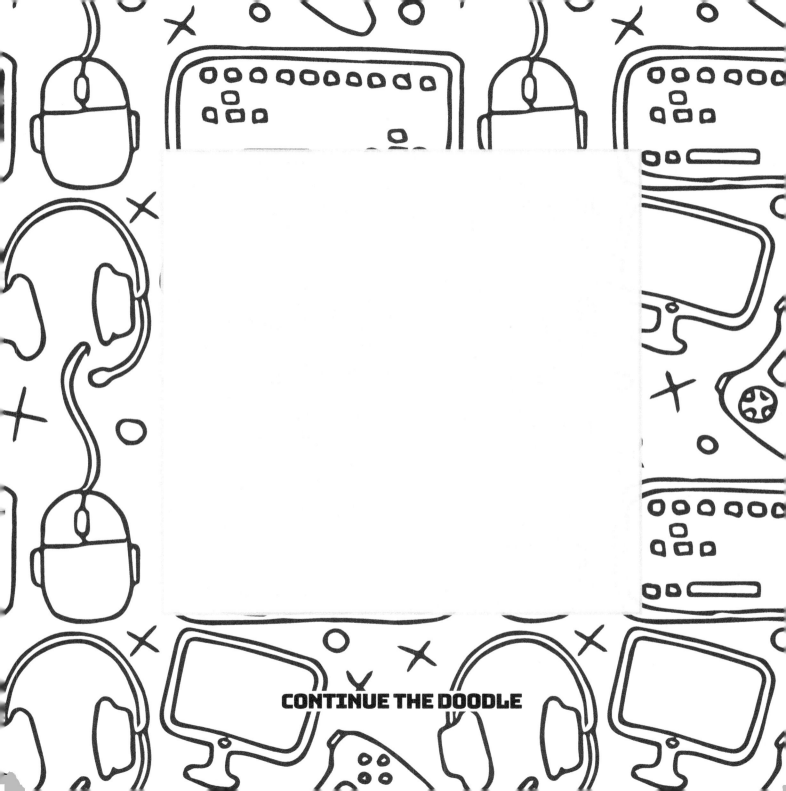

CONTINUE THE DOODLE

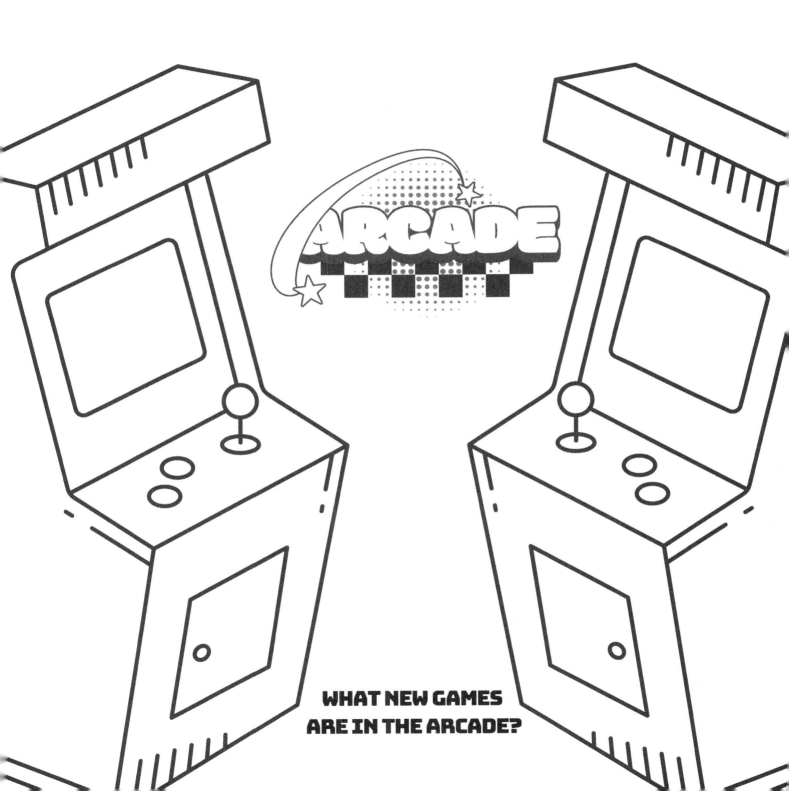

WHAT NEW GAMES
ARE IN THE ARCADE?

DOODLE YOUR OWN PINBALL GAME

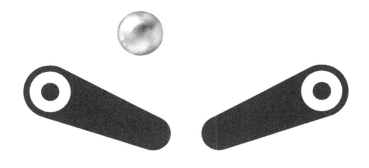

DOODLE A CHALLENGE

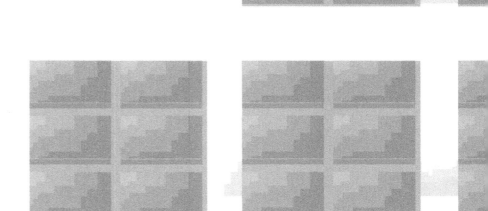

DOODLE A FLOATING ISLAND LEVEL

COLLECT THEM ALL!
COLOR THEM ALL!

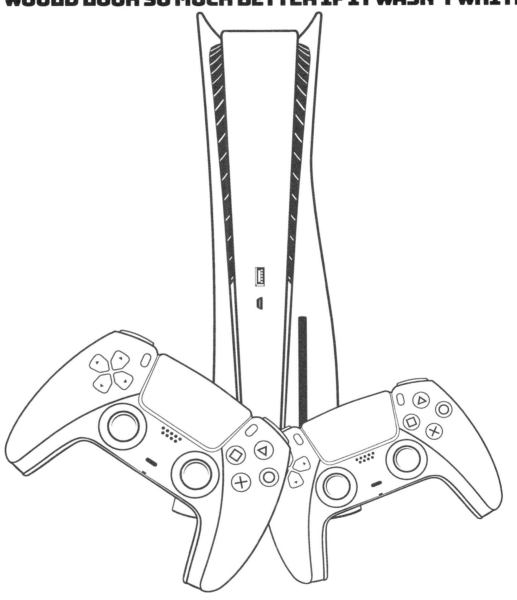

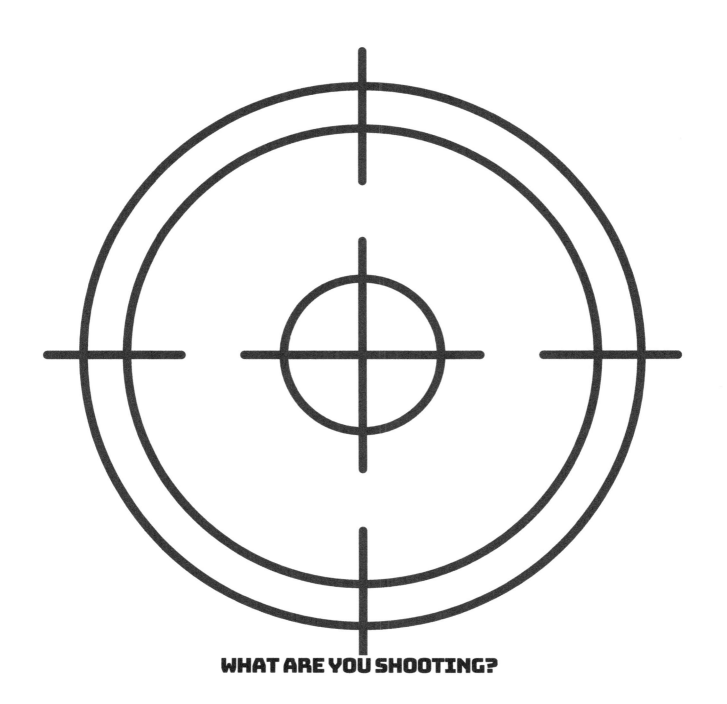

WHAT ARE YOU SHOOTING?

COLLECT THEM ALL! COLOR THEM ALL!

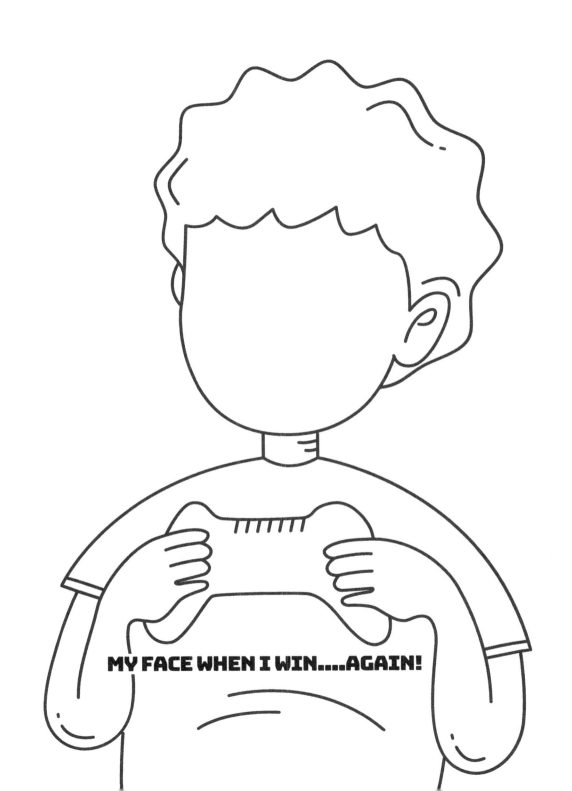

DESIGN YOUR OWN ROBOT

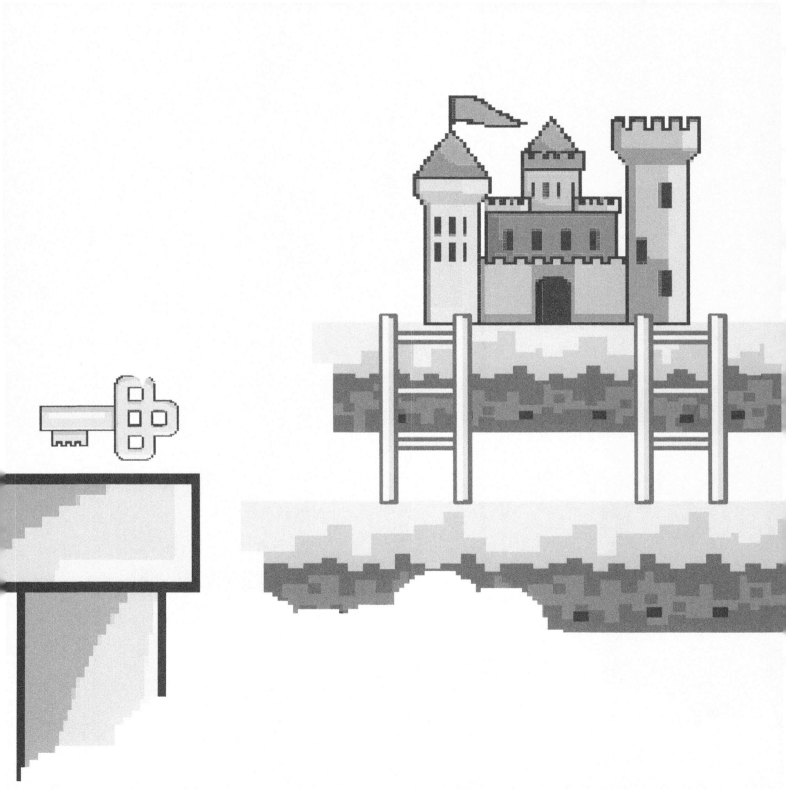

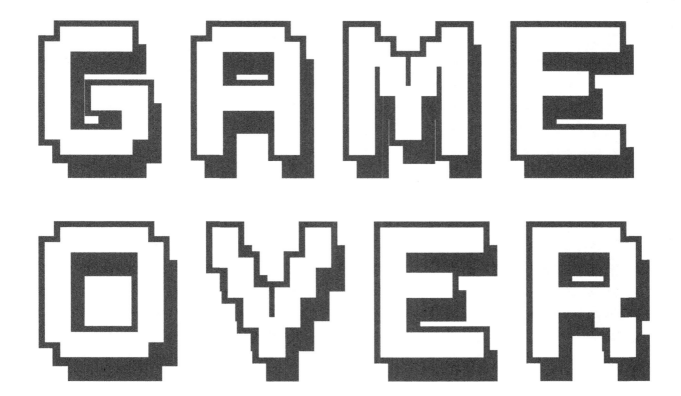

OTHER BOOKS BY
WOMZIZ

FLUFFY AND PLUSHIE ORIGINALS

Immerse yourself in 50+ unique designs inspired by iconic plush toys. Perfect for a plushie lover, ready to color any stress away.

EASTER GAMER

The perfect Easter Basket Stuffer full of 50+ unique designs inspired by iconic gaming moments,! Perfect for a gamer, ready to color in and doodle any stress away this Easter. .

Made in United States
Orlando, FL
18 April 2025

60514584R00063